GO QUIZ YOURSELF ON
DINOSAURS

T0014567

IZZI
HOWELL

CRABTREE
PUBLISHING COMPANY
WWW.CRABTREEBOOKS.COM

CRABTREE
PUBLISHING COMPANY
WWW.CRABTREEBOOKS.COM

Author: Izzi Howell
Editorial director: Kathy Middleton
Series editor: Izzi Howell
Editor: Crystal Sikkens
Proofreader: Wendy Scavuzzo
Series design: Rocket Design (East Anglia) Ltd
Prepress technician: Katherine Berti
Print coordinator: Katherine Berti

Every effort has been made to clear copyright.
Should there be any inadvertent omission,
please apply to the publisher for rectification.

The website addresses (URLs) included in this book were
valid at the time of going to press. However, it is possible that
contents or addresses may have changed since the publication
of this book. No responsibility for any such changes can be
accepted by either the author or the publisher.

All facts and statistics were correct at the time of press.

Picture acknowledgements: Getty: VasjaKoman cover r,
title page r, 20c and 22l, Nadzeya_Dzivakova 5t, 6, 20b, 21t,
22r, 23l and 25t, johnnylemonseed 14l, AdrianHillman 26–
27b and 28–29, Yevhenii Dorofieiev 32t, vector 32c; NASA/
JPL 8b; Shutterstock: dedMazay cover l and title page l,
Amanita Silvicora 4, HappyPictures 5c, 6, 10 and 46, T-Kot
5b, Kapustina Alexandra 7, 10 and 46, Elegant Solution 7,
10 and 46, tn-prints 7, 10 and 46, ideyweb 7, 11 and 47,
Zakharchenko Anna 7, 11 and 47, NotionPic 7, 11 and 47,
bonezboyz 6, 11 and 47, LuckyStep 6, Iconic Bestiary 7,
Chalintra.B 7, Sudowoodo 8t, TrishaMcmillan, Nadezhda
Shpiiakina and Egret77 9b, Macrovector 12–13, 16–17 and
27t, ideyweb 12b and 17t, Gluiki 14–15c, Nadzin 14br,
Rvector 15tl, Hennadii H 15tr, Pretty Vectors 15b, Teguh
Mujiono 18t and 42, Arkela 18b, maxicam 19tl, Taras Dubov
19tr, asantosg 19c, Alfmaler 19b and 23r, Gaynore 20t and
22c, Nadezhda Shpiiakina 21c and 23c, udaix 21b and 43c,
Eduard Radu 24t, Jaroslav Moravcik 24b, Tatyana Dunaeva
25t, KatePilko 25b and 48, Ton Bangkeaw 26t, Alyoha 27c,
Olga_Belova 30, Maquiladora, AnnstasAg and Nadzin 31t
and 34–35, AKKHARAT JARUSILAWONG 31b, Nadya_Art
32b, N.MacTavish 33l, SLKi, Azimuth_A and StockVector 33,
NoPainNoGain 36–37c, GraphicsRF 36b and 41t, graphic-
line 37t, Best Vector Elements 38b, rvika 39t, VectorPot 39c
and 40b, Yauhen Paleski 39b and 42br, nikiteev_konstantin
43t, Blan-k 43b; Techtype 14bl, 37b, 38t, 40t, 41bl. All
design elements from Shutterstock.

Library and Archives Canada Cataloguing in Publication

Title: Go quiz yourself on dinosaurs / Izzi Howell.
Other titles: Dinosaurs
Names: Howell, Izzi, author.
Description: Series statement: Go quiz yourself |
  Includes index.
Identifiers: Canadiana (print) 20200358022 |
  Canadiana (ebook) 20200358073 |
  ISBN 9781427128720 (hardcover) |
  ISBN 9781427128782 (softcover) |
  ISBN 9781427128843 (HTML)
Subjects: LCSH: Dinosaurs–Juvenile literature. |
  LCSH: Dinosaurs–Problems, exercises, etc.–
  Juvenile literature.
Classification: LCC QE861.5 .H69 2021 | DDC j567.9–dc23

Library of Congress Cataloging-in-Publication Data

Names: Howell, Izzi, author.
Title: Go quiz yourself on dinosaurs / Izzi Howell.
Description: New York : Crabtree Publishing Company, 2021.
  | Series: Go quiz yourself | First published in Great Britain
  in 2020 by Wayland. | Audience: Ages 9-14+ | Audience:
  Grades 4-6 | Summary: "Read about the different kinds of
  dinosaurs and other prehistoric creatures that lived long
  ago. Find out how they lived and died, how only their
  fossils remain, and much more. Then see if you can answer
  questions, such as: Why did the dinosaurs become extinct?
  Which dinosaur had the smallest brain? What can we learn
  from dinosaur footprints?"-- Provided by publisher.
Identifiers: LCCN 2020046069 (print) |
  LCCN 2020046070 (ebook) |
  ISBN 9781427128720 (hardcover) |
  ISBN 9781427128782 (paperback) |
  ISBN 9781427128843 (ebook)
Subjects: LCSH: Dinosaurs--Juvenile literature.
Classification: LCC QE861.5 .H69 2021 (print) |
  LCC QE861.5 (ebook) | DDC 567.9--dc23
LC record available at https://lccn.loc.gov/2020046069
LC ebook record available at https://lccn.loc.gov/2020046070

Crabtree Publishing Company

www.crabtreebooks.com   1-800-387-7650

Published by Crabtree Publishing Company in 2021

First published in Great Britain in 2020 by Wayland
Copyright ©Hodder and Stoughton Limited, 2020

**Published
in Canada
Crabtree Publishing**
616 Welland Ave.
St. Catharines, Ontario
L2M 5V6

**Published in
the United States
Crabtree Publishing**
347 Fifth Ave
Suite 1402-145
New York, NY 10016

Printed in the U.S.A./122020/CG20201014

CONTENTS

HOW TO USE THIS BOOK

This book is packed full of amazing facts and statistics. After you've finished reading a section, test yourself with questions on the following pages. Check your answers on pages 44-45 and see if you're a quizmaster or if you need to quiz it again! When you've finished, test your friends and family to find out who's the ultimate quiz champion!

WHAT IS A DINOSAUR?

Dinosaurs were the main land animals on Earth for millions of years. Although dinosaurs eventually became extinct, we have learned a huge amount about them from the fossils **they left behind.**

TERRIBLE LIZARDS

The word "dinosaur" comes from two Greek words—*deinos*, meaning terrible, and *sauros,* meaning reptile or lizard. Dinosaurs were a type of reptile, but they aren't related to modern reptiles. Birds are actually the closest living relative to dinosaurs.

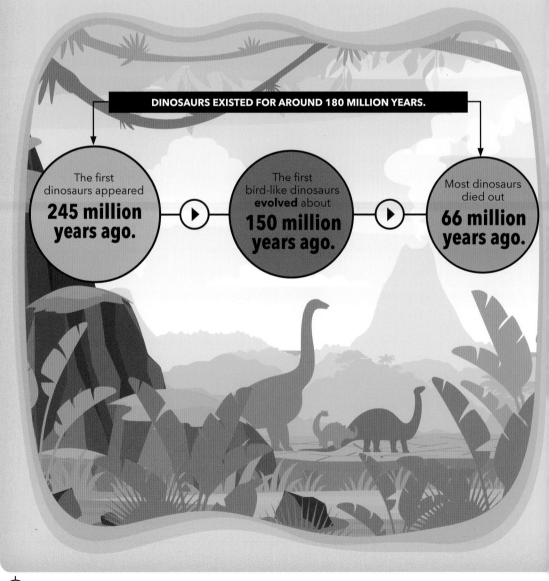

DINOSAURS EXISTED FOR AROUND 180 MILLION YEARS.

The first dinosaurs appeared
245 million years ago.

▶

The first bird-like dinosaurs **evolved** about
150 million years ago.

▶

Most dinosaurs died out
66 million years ago.

DINOSAUR ANATOMY

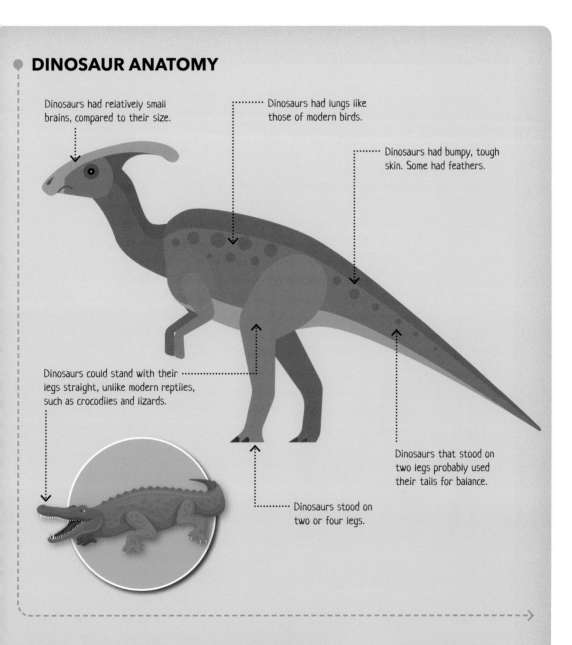

Dinosaurs had relatively small brains, compared to their size.

Dinosaurs had lungs like those of modern birds.

Dinosaurs had bumpy, tough skin. Some had feathers.

Dinosaurs could stand with their legs straight, unlike modern reptiles, such as crocodiles and lizards.

Dinosaurs that stood on two legs probably used their tails for balance.

Dinosaurs stood on two or four legs.

OVER TIME

We often think of all dinosaurs living together at the same time. However, that's not accurate. Different species of dinosaurs lived at different times, millions of years apart. Over time, dinosaurs evolved into new dinosaur species and replaced each other.

LIFE THROUGH TIME

Life on Earth started hundreds of millions of years before the dinosaurs. Dinosaurs lived in the Mesozoic Era, but there were many other eras before and after the dinosaurs.

ERAS

An era is a section of Earth's history based on the age of layers of **sedimentary rock**. Each layer of rock contains fossils of species that lived at that time. Plants and animals were buried by **sediment** and turned into rock over time (see pages 42-43). Eras are divided into **periods**.

Although it looks like a plant, this species, *Charnia*, is actually thought to be the first animal.

Precambrian Eon
(4.6 billion years ago to 541 million years ago)

This period began when Earth started to form.

The first simple-celled organisms appeared 3,600 million years ago, while the first animals appeared 600 million years ago in the oceans.

Allosaurus (AL-oh-saw-rus)

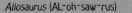

Coelophysis (seel-OH-fie-sis) was a late Triassic dinosaur. Dinosaurs from that period were smaller than later dinosaurs.

Mesozoic Era

Triassic Period
(252 to 201 million years ago)

Most of the land on Earth was one supercontinent called Pangaea, which was surrounded by one ocean.

The first dinosaurs, flying reptiles, and marine reptiles appeared, alongside the first very small mammals.

Jurassic Period
(201 to 145 million years ago)

Pangaea split apart into separate continents.

Large sauropod dinosaurs and carnivorous theropod dinosaurs appeared (see pages 12-13).

The first birds evolved from dinosaurs.

Mesonychid (mess-ON-ee-kid) was a Paleogene mammal.

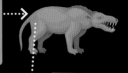

Cenozoic Era

Triceratops (tri-SERRA-tops) lived toward the end of the Cretaceous Period.

Cretaceous Period
(145 to 66 million years ago)

All dinosaurs, apart from bird-like dinosaurs, along with many other prehistoric animals died in a mass extinction at the end of the Cretaceous Period.

Paleogene Period
(66 to 23 million years ago)

The death of dinosaurs allowed large numbers of different mammal species to develop, including many giant mammals.

Some mammals lived in the ocean (whales and dolphins), while others lived in the trees (primates).

Endoceras

coral

trilobite

Paleozoic Era

Ordovician Period
(485 to 443 million years ago)

The climate on Earth warmed and sea levels rose.

The first fish evolved in the ocean and the first simple plants (with no roots, stems, or leaves) grew on land.

Silurian Period
(443 to 419 million years ago)

The first fish with jaws evolved in the ocean.

On land, plants developed veins that carried water around the plant.

Cambrian Period
(541 to 485 million years ago)

Many animals evolved in the oceans during an event called the Cambrian explosion.

There was no life on land yet.

Devonian Period
(419 to 359 million years ago)

This period is sometimes called the "Age of Fishes," as many types of fish evolved.

The first four-legged amphibians evolved from fish and began to adapt to life on land.

Dimetrodon (die-MET-trow-don) is often mistaken for a dinosaur, but it was actually a synapsid.

Dunkleosteus

Carboniferous Period
(359 to 299 million years ago)

Many species of invertebrate evolved, including dragonflies and grasshoppers.

Amphibians developed further and the first reptiles appeared.

Permian Period
(299 to 252 million years ago)

Different reptile species evolved and the first synapsids (mammal-like reptiles that eventually became mammals) appeared.

The Permian Period ended with a mass extinction, in which 90 percent of species were wiped out.

Neogene Period
(23 to 2.6 million years ago)

The ancestors of humans evolved during this period, at least 4.5 million years ago.

Most mammals and birds evolved to the forms that we know today.

Quaternary Period
(2.6 million years ago to present day)

The first humans (_Homo sapiens_) evolved around 300,000 years ago.

Human civilization began during the Stone Age.

THE END OF THE DINOSAURS

No one knows exactly why most of the dinosaurs became extinct around 66 million years ago. The most widely accepted idea is that a massive asteroid crashed into Earth and disrupted the climate.

THE ASTEROID THEORY

When the asteroid hit Earth, the impact created huge dust clouds that filled the skies. Everything on Earth became darker and colder. Plants died without sunlight, which meant that many **herbivores** starved. This ended the food supply of their predators, the **carnivores**.

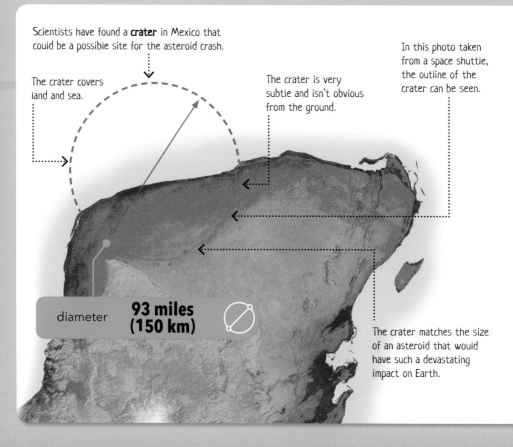

Scientists have found a **crater** in Mexico that could be a possible site for the asteroid crash.

The crater covers land and sea.

The crater is very subtle and isn't obvious from the ground.

In this photo taken from a space shuttle, the outline of the crater can be seen.

diameter **93 miles (150 km)**

The crater matches the size of an asteroid that would have such a devastating impact on Earth.

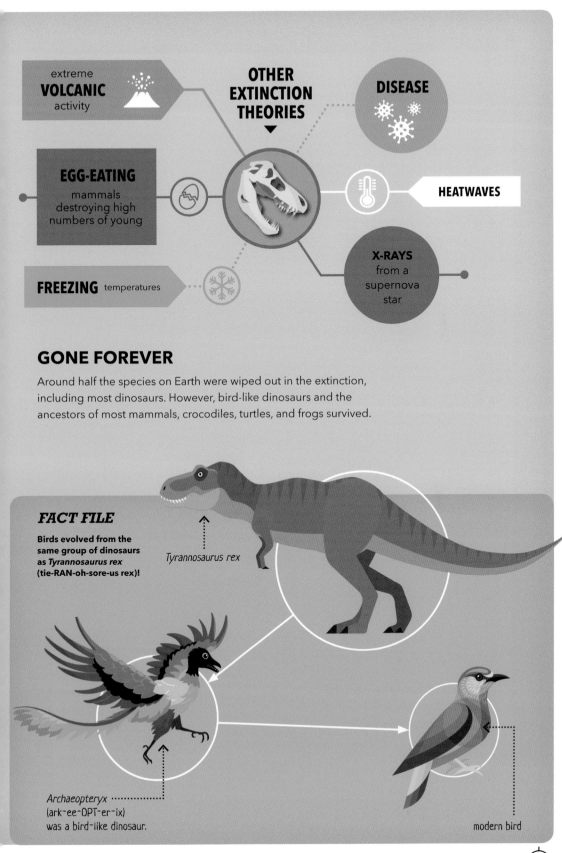

OTHER EXTINCTION THEORIES ▼

extreme **VOLCANIC** activity

DISEASE

EGG-EATING mammals destroying high numbers of young

HEATWAVES

FREEZING temperatures

X-RAYS from a supernova star

GONE FOREVER

Around half the species on Earth were wiped out in the extinction, including most dinosaurs. However, bird-like dinosaurs and the ancestors of most mammals, crocodiles, turtles, and frogs survived.

FACT FILE

Birds evolved from the same group of dinosaurs as *Tyrannosaurus rex* (tie-RAN-oh-sore-us rex)!

Tyrannosaurus rex

Archaeopteryx (ark-ee-OPT-er-ix) was a bird-like dinosaur.

modern bird

GO QUIZ YOURSELF!

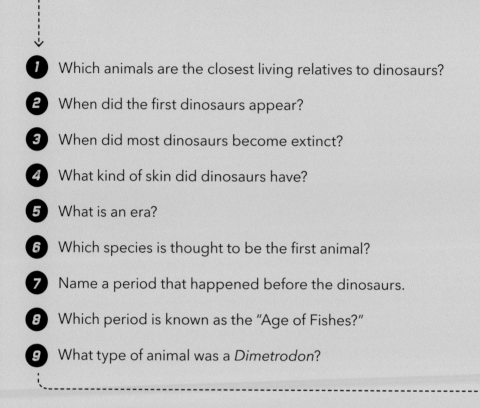

1 Which animals are the closest living relatives to dinosaurs?

2 When did the first dinosaurs appear?

3 When did most dinosaurs become extinct?

4 What kind of skin did dinosaurs have?

5 What is an era?

6 Which species is thought to be the first animal?

7 Name a period that happened before the dinosaurs.

8 Which period is known as the "Age of Fishes?"

9 What type of animal was a *Dimetrodon*?

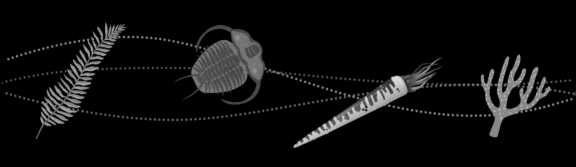

- - - - - -> **10** What was Pangaea?

11 In which period did the first birds evolve from dinosaurs?

12 When did the Jurassic Period begin and end?

13 In which period did *Triceratops* live?

14 How many years ago did humans (*Homo sapiens*) evolve?

15 In which country have scientists found a possible asteroid crash site?

16 Aside from the asteroid crash, name two other theories about dinosaur extinction.

17 Name an animal that survived the extinction event.

TYPES OF DINOSAURS

Dinosaurs can be divided into two main groups: saurischians and ornithischians. These groups can be split up further into many other types of dinosaurs.

Saurischians

★ means "lizard hipped"

★ includes carnivores and herbivores

Sauropods

★ huge herbivores

★ walked on four legs

★ some of the largest of all the dinosaurs

★ long necks and tails

Theropods

★ carnivores

★ walked on two legs and had short front limbs

★ three forward-facing toes, like the feet of many modern birds

Tyrannosaurus was a theropod from the Late Cretaceous. Its name means "tyrant lizard."

Bird-like dinosaurs

★ evolved from small theropods

★ moved into trees looking for food or protection

★ ancestors of modern birds

Brachiosaurus (BRAK-ee-oh-sore-us) was a Late Jurassic sauropod. It was 98 feet (30 m) long— nearly as long as 2 ten-pin bowling lanes!

Archaeopteryx was a Late Jurassic bird-like dinosaur that was around the size of a crow.

Dinosaur ancestors

★ lived in the Middle and Late Triassic Periods

★ were small and walked on two legs

Ornithischians

★ means "bird hipped" (although birds are actually descended from saurischians)

★ all herbivores

★ most had beaks

Ankylosaurus

★ armored dinosaurs

★ flat, bony plates on their backs and sides for defense

Ankylosaurus (an-KIE-loh-sore-us) lived in the Late Cretaceous. It had a bony club at the end of its tail.

Ornithopods

★ early, smaller ornithopods walked on two feet

★ as they got larger and heavier, they started to use their front limbs to support their weight as well

Iguanodon (ig-WHA-noh-don) was an ornithopod from the Early Cretaceous. It was one of the first species of dinosaur to be identified.

Ceratopsians

★ horns on the head

★ huge bony frills at the back of the head

Triceratops, from the Late Cretaceous, had a relatively small frill compared to other ceratopsians.

Stegosaurs

★ diamond-shaped bony plates along the back, probably for defense or to attract a mate

★ slow-moving as their back legs were much longer than their front legs, so they couldn't run on all fours

Stegosaurus (STEG-oh-SORE-us) lived in the Late Jurassic. It had a spiked tail for defense.

Pachycephalosaurus

★ thick bone at the front of their skulls, which may have allowed them to smash their heads together to fight, just as some rams do today

★ walked on two legs

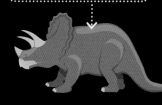

The skull of the Pachycephalosaurus (pack-i-KEF-al-oh-sore-rus), which lived in the Late Cretaceous, was 20 times thicker than a normal dinosaur skull.

RECORD-BREAKING DINOSAURS

18 m

Dinosaurs were some of the most incredible animals ever to live on Earth. They reached record-breaking sizes and had amazing body parts.

TALLEST DINOSAUR

At 60 feet (18 m) tall, *Sauroposeidon* (sore-oh-poss-I-den) was the tallest dinosaur. It was as tall as 3 giraffes on top of each other. Its huge height was mainly made up of its enormous neck.

LARGEST DINOSAUR

The *Patagotitan* (pat-ag-o-TIGHT-an) weighed more than 66 tons (60 metric tons), which is about the same as 12 African elephants! This makes it the largest dinosaur, as well as the largest recorded land animal. However, **paleontologists** have never found a complete *Patagotitan* skeleton, so its size is an estimate based on individual bones. One of its thigh bones measures 8 feet (2.5 m) long!

MOST HORNS

Kosmoceratops (cos-mo-SERRA-tops) had 15 horns and spikes on its head! There were 10 on its frill, 1 above each eye, 1 on each cheek, and 1 on its nose. Its horns were probably used to attract a mate.

LONGEST CREST

Parasaurolophus (pa-ra-saw-ROL-off-us) had a 3-foot (1-m)-long crest, which measured as long as the skull itself. Tubes inside the crest might have been used as a trumpet to make sounds to communicate.

SMALLEST DINOSAUR

Compsognathus (comp-sog-NATH-us) was one of the smallest known dinosaurs, at roughly the size of a chicken! It was also possibly one of the fastest dinosaurs with estimated speeds of more than 37 mph (60 kph).

ACTUAL SIZE OF *STEGOSAURUS* BRAIN!

SMALLEST BRAIN

Dinosaurs had comparatively small brains and *Stegosaurus* had one of the smallest brains of all. Its brain was around the size of a lime, even though *Stegosaurus* was 30 feet (9 m) long! Most of the space in its head was taken up by biting muscles.

scale size of brain!

GO QUIZ YOURSELF!

18 What are the two main groups of dinosaur?

19 What diet did theropods have?

20 What does *Tyrannosaurus* mean?

21 Name a bird-like dinosaur.

22 How long was *Brachiosaurus*?

23 What type of dinosaur was *Iguanodon*?

24 Why did *Ankylosaurus* have flat, bony plates on their back and sides?

25 Why did *Stegosaurus* move slowly?

26 Which *Pachycephalosaurus* bone was particularly thick?

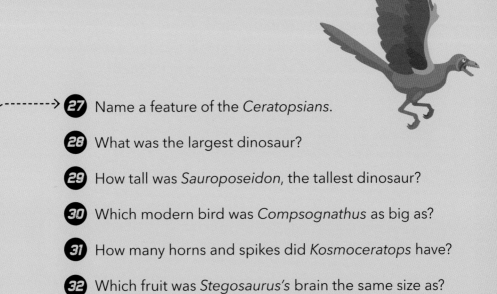

27 Name a feature of the *Ceratopsians*.

28 What was the largest dinosaur?

29 How tall was *Sauroposeidon*, the tallest dinosaur?

30 Which modern bird was *Compsognathus* as big as?

31 How many horns and spikes did *Kosmoceratops* have?

32 Which fruit was *Stegosaurus's* brain the same size as?

33 Which dinosaur had the longest crest?

34 How did *Parasaurolophus* possibly use the tubes inside its crest?

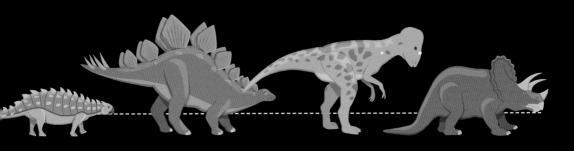

DIET

Different dinosaurs had different diets; some were carnivores, while others were herbivores and omnivores. The easiest way to identify a dinosaur's diet is by looking at its teeth.

huge spiked teeth

strong jaw

CARNIVORE TEETH

Carnivores had blade-like, **serrated** teeth that could cut through flesh and break it down into smaller chunks. Their teeth and jaws were strong so they could crack through the bones of their prey. Some carnivores had pointed teeth and long jaws to grab fish out of the water.

sharp beak

teeth in the cheek for chewing food

HERBIVORE TEETH

Many herbivores had sharp front teeth or beaks for grabbing leaves. Some had serrated teeth to slice through leaves. Others had peg-like teeth, which acted like a rake, to strip leaves off plants.

TOO MANY TEETH!

The herbivore *Edmontosaurus* (ed-MON-toe-sore-us) had more than 1,000 teeth! Its teeth broke leaves down into pulp in its mouth.

SHARP FOREVER

Dinosaurs' teeth constantly fell out and were replaced throughout their life, so they never became dull.

OMNIVORES

Omnivores had a mixture of different types of teeth. Some would have been sharp for cutting through meat, while others were more suited to breaking down plants.

sharp teeth for cutting through meat

flat teeth for breaking down plants

SWALLOWING STONES

Some sauropods swallowed stones to help them digest the tough plants they ate. The stones sat in their stomachs and ground down any food they swallowed. Paleontologists have found these stones inside the stomachs of fossilized dinosaurs.

APEX PREDATORS

Some carnivores were apex predators. This means they were at the top of the food chain and had no natural predators. However, smaller carnivores were the prey of larger dinosaurs and other predators, such as pterosaurs (see pages 30–31).

ATTACK AND DEFENSE

Fierce carnivorous dinosaurs were skilled predators and were adapted for deadly attacks. However, their prey also developed ways to defend themselves and fight back.

DEADLY DINOSAUR ATTACKS

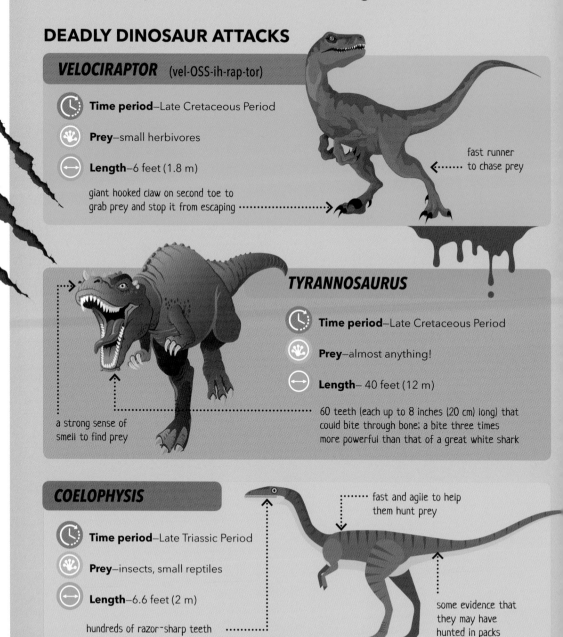

VELOCIRAPTOR (vel-OSS-ih-rap-tor)

Time period—Late Cretaceous Period

Prey—small herbivores

Length—6 feet (1.8 m)

giant hooked claw on second toe to grab prey and stop it from escaping

fast runner to chase prey

TYRANNOSAURUS

Time period—Late Cretaceous Period

Prey—almost anything!

Length— 40 feet (12 m)

a strong sense of smell to find prey

60 teeth (each up to 8 inches (20 cm) long) that could bite through bone; a bite three times more powerful than that of a great white shark

COELOPHYSIS

Time period—Late Triassic Period

Prey—insects, small reptiles

Length—6.6 feet (2 m)

hundreds of razor-sharp teeth

fast and agile to help them hunt prey

some evidence that they may have hunted in packs

INCREDIBLE DINOSAUR DEFENSE

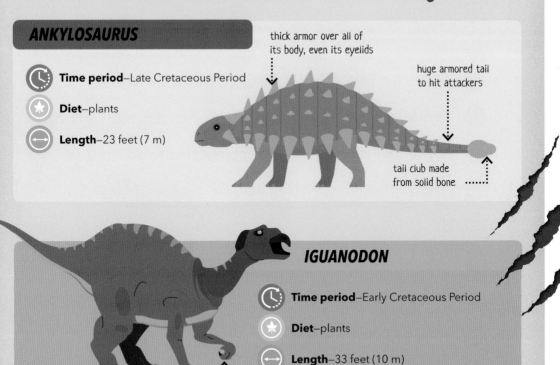

ANKYLOSAURUS

🕐 **Time period**–Late Cretaceous Period

✳ **Diet**–plants

↔ **Length**–23 feet (7 m)

thick armor over all of its body, even its eyelids

huge armored tail to hit attackers

tail club made from solid bone

IGUANODON

🕐 **Time period**–Early Cretaceous Period

✳ **Diet**–plants

↔ **Length**–33 feet (10 m)

large spikes on its thumbs to stab attackers
(the spikes could also be used to cut through plants)

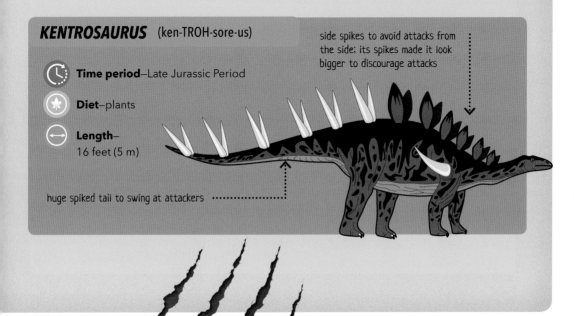

KENTROSAURUS (ken-TROH-sore-us)

🕐 **Time period**–Late Jurassic Period

✳ **Diet**–plants

↔ **Length**–
16 feet (5 m)

side spikes to avoid attacks from the side; its spikes made it look bigger to discourage attacks

huge spiked tail to swing at attackers

GO QUIZ YOURSELF!

35 What is the easiest way to identify a dinosaur's diet?

36 What kind of teeth did carnivorous dinosaurs have?

37 Why did some carnivores have pointed teeth and long jaws?

38 How did peg-like teeth help herbivores gather leaves?

39 Which dinosaur had over 1,000 teeth?

40 Why did dinosaurs' teeth never become dull?

41 Why did sauropods swallow stones?

42 What is an apex predator?

43 How did *Velociraptors'* claws help them hunt?

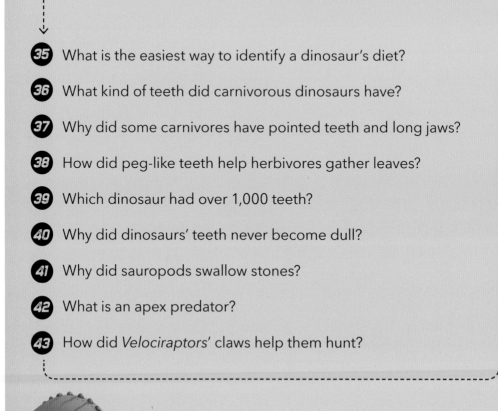

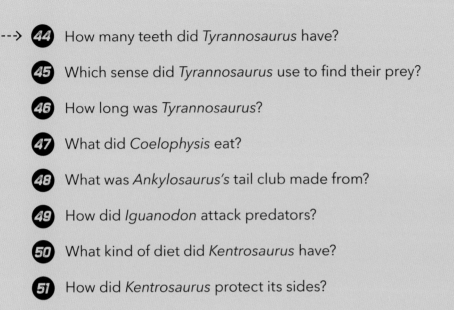

EGGS AND YOUNG

Paleontologists believe that newborn dinosaurs hatched from eggs.

DINOSAUR EGG FACTS

Some dinosaur eggs were
COLORED
and had patterns on them.

The largest dinosaur eggs ever found measure nearly
20 INCHES (51 cm)
in length!

Dinosaur eggs weren't as super-sized as the dinosaurs. For example, an adult *Ampelosaurus* (am-PEL-oh-sore-us) weighed nearly
15,432 POUNDS (7,000 KG),
but its egg only weighed
8.8 POUNDS (4 KG)!

Some dinosaurs laid more than
20 EGGS
in one nest.

Paleontologists have found fossilized dinosaur eggs, nests, and even **embryos**.

These eggs came from a *Hadrosaurus* (HAD-row-sore-us)— a duck-billed dinosaur.

They study what's inside the egg by scanning it or by removing the shell with strong acid.

When the first dinosaur eggs were discovered, people thought they came from giant birds!

NESTS

Different species of dinosaurs built different types of nests. Some were open, while others covered their eggs in soil, sand, or dead plants. Some species of dinosaurs sat on their nests, just like modern birds. Dinosaur nests are often found in raised areas. They may have chosen these places because they were safer. It is possible that they returned to the same place every year to lay their eggs.

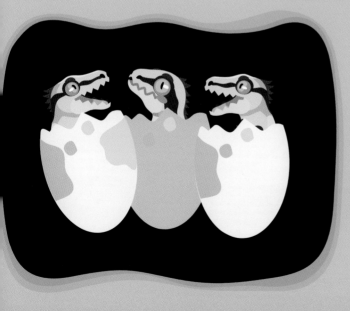

INSIDE THE EGG

Female dinosaurs laid eggs that had been fertilized by a male. One dinosaur embryo developed inside each egg, getting nutrients from the yolk. When the dinosaur young were ready, they broke their way out of the eggs. They were probably able to survive on their own and may not have stayed with their parents for long.

LIVING TOGETHER

Paleontologists think that some dinosaurs were social animals. They may have lived and hunted together.

FOOTPRINT CLUES

Fossilized dinosaur footprints provide excellent clues to dinosaur behavior. By tracing the footprints, we can see where they moved and how many dinosaurs travelled together. We can even calculate their speed by measuring the distance between their steps.

ATTACK!

Small carnivores, such as *Coelophysis,* may have also lived in groups and hunted together to bring down larger prey. They probably didn't have any organized tactics—they just all attacked at the same time.

HERBIVORE HERDS

Dinosaur footprints reveal that some sauropods and other herbivores, such as *Diplodocus* (di-PLOD-uh-cus), travelled in large **herds**. There was safety in numbers, as some could eat while others kept watch for predators. Large groups were less likely to be targeted by carnivores, so the young and injured were protected.

DINOSAUR GRAVEYARD

Around 1,000 *Coelophysis* skeletons have been found in one quarry in New Mexico, USA, which suggests that a very large group lived there together.

GO QUIZ YOURSELF!

52 How were dinosaurs born?

53 What did dinosaur eggs look like?

54 How much did an *Ampelosaurus* egg weigh?

55 How long are the largest dinosaur eggs ever found?

56 How do paleontologists study what's inside fossilized dinosaur eggs?

57 What did people first think when they found dinosaur eggs?

58 Describe a type of dinosaur nest.

59 Why did dinosaurs often build their nests in raised areas?

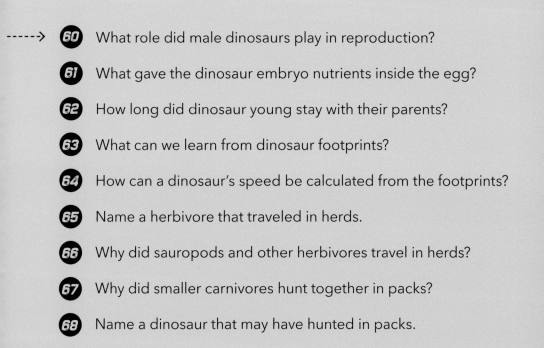

-----> **60** What role did male dinosaurs play in reproduction?

61 What gave the dinosaur embryo nutrients inside the egg?

62 How long did dinosaur young stay with their parents?

63 What can we learn from dinosaur footprints?

64 How can a dinosaur's speed be calculated from the footprints?

65 Name a herbivore that traveled in herds.

66 Why did sauropods and other herbivores travel in herds?

67 Why did smaller carnivores hunt together in packs?

68 Name a dinosaur that may have hunted in packs.

PTEROSAURS

Pterosaurs (TEH-ruh-sores) were flying prehistoric reptiles.
They weren't actually dinosaurs, but they lived at the same time.

FIRST FLIERS

Pterosaurs were the first **vertebrates** to fly and the first animals to evolve flight after insects.
Their wings were thin and stretched from their shoulder to their ankle. Pterosaurs may have had
fur and feathers. Some were probably **warm-blooded** (see page 33), unlike modern reptiles.

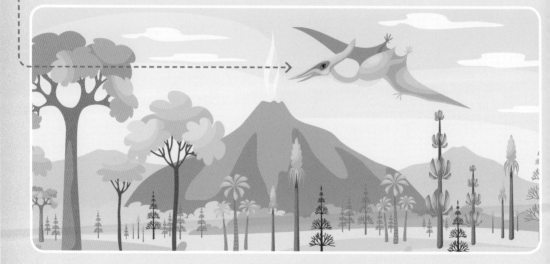

BIG AND SMALL

The first pterosaurs were small—around the size of pigeons.
Over millions of years, they evolved to be much larger. Their
tails became shorter and their heads and limbs became longer.

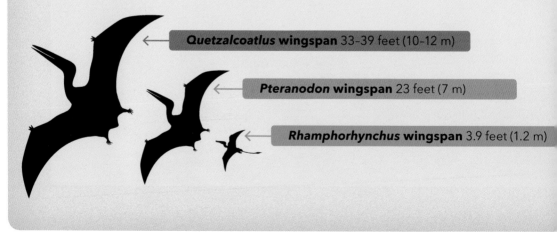

Quetzalcoatlus wingspan 33–39 feet (10–12 m)

Pteranodon wingspan 23 feet (7 m)

Rhamphorhynchus wingspan 3.9 feet (1.2 m)

Quetzalcoatlus (KWETZ-al-co-AT-lis)

★ This pterosaur lived in the Cretaceous Period.

★ *Quetzalcoatlus* was one of the largest-known flying animals of all time.

★ At 16.4 feet (5 m) tall, it was nearly as tall as a giraffe.

★ Its giant jaws measured 8.2 feet (2.5 m) long.

Pteranodon (ter-AN-a-don)

★ This pterosaur lived in the Cretaceous Period.

★ Its long, pointed crest was probably used to attract a mate.

★ It had a long, toothless jaw.

★ More *Pteranodon* fossils have been found than any other pterosaur.

Rhamphorhynchus (ram-fur-INK-us)

★ This pterosaur lived in the Jurassic Period.

★ It only measured 20 inches (51 cm) long.

★ *Rhamphorhynchus* had a diamond-shaped rudder at the tip of its tail.

★ Its teeth angled forward to grab fish out of the water.

THE END OF THE PTEROSAURS

Pterosaurs died out 66 million years ago, at the same time as the dinosaurs. They have no living descendants.

Paleontologists have learned a lot about pterosaurs from fossil remains. ·····>

SEA CREATURES

During the Mesozoic Era, many types of aquatic reptiles lived in the ocean. These creatures were related to the dinosaurs, but they weren't dinosaurs.

Ichthyosaurs (IK-thee-oh-sores)

★ Ichthyosaurs lived throughout the whole Mesozoic Era.

★ They looked like dolphins or porpoises.

★ They had very large eyes, which may have meant they had good eyesight to spot predators, such as plesiosaurs.

Mosasaurs (MOZE-ah-sores)

★ Mosasaurs lived in the Cretaceous Period.

★ They had snake-like bodies with large, strong flippers and long tails.

★ Mosasaurs are related to modern monitor lizards.

Monitor lizard

COMPETITION

Different species of ichthyosaurs, mosasaurs, and plesiosaurs lived at the same time. They competed with each other for food, such as fish, **ammonites**, and cuttlefish. They also preyed on and ate each other, particularly young or weak animals.

ammonite

fish

cuttlefish

Plesiosaurs (PLEEZ-i-oh-sores)

★ **Plesiosaurs lived from the Late Triassic Period to the Late Cretaceous Period.**

★ **In the Cretaceous Period, plesiosaurs reached huge sizes, measuring 39-49 feet (12-15 m), more than half of which was their head and neck.**

★ **One species of plesiosaur is thought to have had the most powerful bite of any animal.**

UNUSUAL REPTILES

Unlike modern reptiles, there is evidence that these aquatic reptiles were warm-blooded. They maintained their own body heat, rather than relying on their surroundings to control their temperature. They also gave birth to live young, unlike modern reptiles.

GO QUIZ YOURSELF!

69 Were pterosaurs dinosaurs?

70 Describe the wings of a pterosaur.

71 What size were the first pterosaurs?

72 How large was the wingspan of a *Quetzalcoatlus*?

73 When did *Quetzalcoatlus* live?

74 Why did *Pteranodon* have a crest?

75 How long was *Rhamphorhynchus*?

76 What did *Rhamphorhynchus* have at the end of its tail?

77 When did the pterosaurs die out?

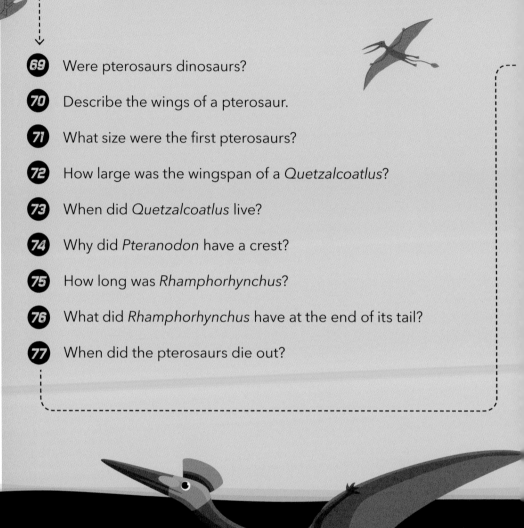

78 Which type of prehistoric sea creature looked like a dolphin?

79 Why did ichthyosaurs have large eyes?

80 When did the first plesiosaurs appear?

81 How long could the biggest plesiosaurs grow?

82 Describe the body of a mosasaur.

83 Which modern animal is related to mosasaurs?

84 What did prehistoric sea reptiles eat?

85 Name one way in which prehistoric sea reptiles were different from modern reptiles.

AMPHIBIANS

Before the dinosaurs, amphibians were one of the first four-limbed animals to walk on land. Their name comes from Greek meaning "living a double life," as they usually live both in water and on land.

WATER TO LAND

Amphibians evolved from fish in the Devonian Period. Some fish had four strong fins that they used as legs to crawl along the ground. They began to pull themselves onto land. They used primitive lungs to breathe air, rather than using **gills** like fish.

Tiktaalik (tick-TAH-lik)

★ *Tiktaalik* was a species between fish and amphibians that lived in the Devonian Period.

★ It had gills and lungs.

★ It used its long fins for swimming or to walk on mud.

★ It had a large pelvis that allowed it to walk as well as swim.

★ It measured up to 9 feet (2.7 m) long.

WATER AND LAND

Over time, amphibians evolved to be able to spend more time out of the water. However, they still had to return to the water from time to time to keep their skin moist and lay their soft eggs. Eventually, reptiles would evolve to not require either of these things, as they grew scaly, dry skin and laid eggs with hard shells on land.

THROUGH TIME

At the time of the first amphibians, there were very few vertebrates on land. Amphibians had plenty of food to eat, including plants and insects, and fish from the water. Later, during the Mesozoic Era, some species became extinct. Other species survived, including the ancestors of modern reptiles, such as frogs and salamanders.

Eryops (EAR-ee-ops)

★ *Eryops* was a large amphibian from the Permian Period.

★ Measuring 6.6 feet (2 m) long, it was one of the largest land animals at that time.

★ It ate mostly fish and other small animals.

★ Its hip structure from fossils shows that it would have been good at walking on land.

EARLY MAMMALS

The first mammals appeared in the Triassic Period. During the Age of the Dinosaurs, mammals remained small, but afterward, they grew to huge sizes.

MESOZOIC MAMMALS

Most mammals that lived at the same time as the dinosaurs were the size of small rodents, such as rats. They were herbivores or insectivores (ate only insects). There were a few exceptions, such as *Repenomamus* (rep-en-o-MAH-mus), which was roughly the size of a badger and hunted vertebrates, including baby dinosaurs.

EGGS AND YOUNG

Mammals have always fed their young milk, but they developed various forms of giving birth over time. The first mammals laid eggs, like the reptiles they evolved from. Some mammals, such as the platypus and the echidna, still lay eggs today. Later, mammals evolved to give birth to very small, live young, which they kept in pouches like kangaroos do. After that, mammals began to give birth to more developed young, like most do today.

Megazostrodon
(meg-ah-ZOSS-troh-don)

★ *Megazostrodon* lived in the Late Triassic Period.

★ It was one of the first mammals.

★ It was the size of a shrew, around 3.9–4.7 inches (10–12 cm) long, and had a furry body.

★ *Megazostrodon* was nocturnal, probably to avoid reptile predators that were active during the day.

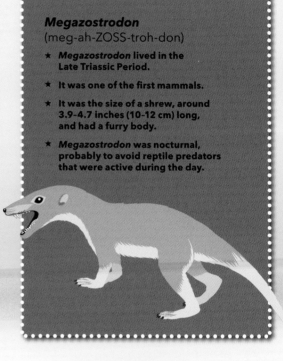

SURVIVAL

Mammals were better equipped to survive the extinction event that we believe to have killed the dinosaurs. They were much smaller, so they didn't need as much food to survive. Their fur coats kept them warm in the cold climate.

GETTING BIGGER

Over time, mammals grew in size and took the place of the dinosaurs as the largest animals on Earth. Huge ancestors of modern animals, such as armadillos, anteaters, and sloths evolved. However, many of these large mammals died out in the last **Ice Age**, around 11,500 years ago.

Megatherium
(meg-ah-THEER-ee-um)

★ *Megatherium* lived during the Quaternary Period, which means that it overlapped with human ancestors.

★ It was related to modern sloths, but was 10 times larger.

★ *Megatherium* weighed up to 4.4 tons (4 metric tons), which is the same as a male Asian elephant.

★ It measured 11.5 feet (3.5 m) tall when standing on its hind legs.

★ It had long arms and large claws to pull branches down to its mouth.

Glyptodon (GLIP-toe-don)

★ *Glyptodon* lived in the Quaternary Period.

★ It was related to modern armadillos, but was much larger. It was around the same size and shape as a Volkswagen Beetle car.

★ *Glyptodon* looked a bit like a turtle, with a huge domed shell made up of bony plates.

★ Its shell measured 4.9 feet (1.5 m) long, making up around half of its length.

★ It had an armored tail with bony spikes that was used as a weapon.

GO QUIZ YOURSELF!

86 Why are amphibians said to lead a double life?

87 In which period did amphibians evolve from fish?

88 How did the first amphibians breathe on land?

89 How did *Tiktaalik* move?

90 Why do amphibians need to return to the water?

91 Name one way in which reptiles have evolved to not need water.

92 How long was *Eryops*?

93 What did *Eryops* eat?

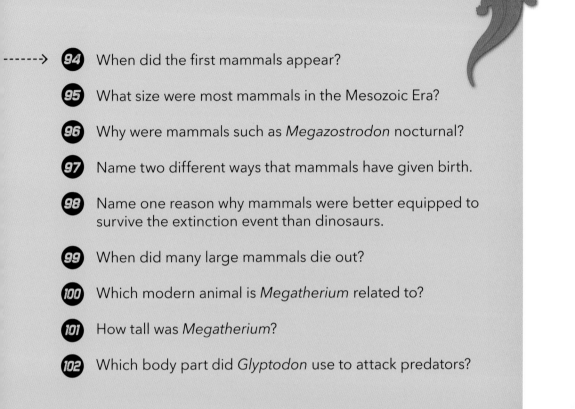

94 When did the first mammals appear?

95 What size were most mammals in the Mesozoic Era?

96 Why were mammals such as *Megazostrodon* nocturnal?

97 Name two different ways that mammals have given birth.

98 Name one reason why mammals were better equipped to survive the extinction event than dinosaurs.

99 When did many large mammals die out?

100 Which modern animal is *Megatherium* related to?

101 How tall was *Megatherium*?

102 Which body part did *Glyptodon* use to attack predators?

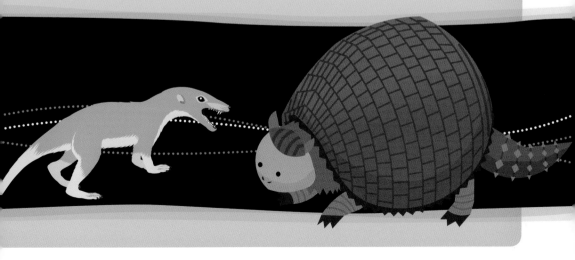

DISCOVERING DINOSAURS

Everything we know about dinosaurs and prehistoric living things comes from fossils (remains preserved in rock).

HISTORY

Up until the late 1600s, no one realized that the animals of today hadn't been around forever, and that different animals, including dinosaurs, even existed. In the 1700s, people started to collect and study fossils and identify dinosaur species. This led to a huge explosion in the understanding of prehistoric life.

Paleontologists use different tools to uncover dinosaur fossils.

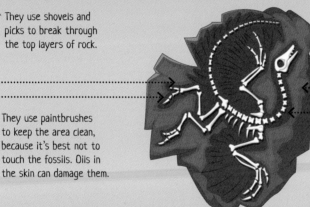

They use shovels and picks to break through the top layers of rock.

As they get closer to the bones, they use smaller rock hammers and tiny knives and chisels.

They use paintbrushes to keep the area clean, because it's best not to touch the fossils. Oils in the skin can damage them.

Paleontologists use glue to stabilize the fossils and stick them back together if they crumble.

HOW ARE FOSSILS FORMED?

Fossils only form when living things are buried by mud or sediment after they die. For this reason, fossils of land animals are rare.

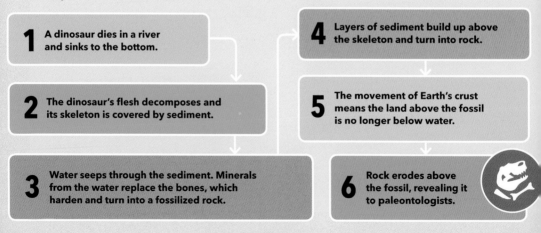

1 A dinosaur dies in a river and sinks to the bottom.

2 The dinosaur's flesh decomposes and its skeleton is covered by sediment.

3 Water seeps through the sediment. Minerals from the water replace the bones, which harden and turn into a fossilized rock.

4 Layers of sediment build up above the skeleton and turn into rock.

5 The movement of Earth's crust means the land above the fossil is no longer below water.

6 Rock erodes above the fossil, revealing it to paleontologists.

TYPES OF FOSSILS

There are many types of fossils.

Preserved in amber **(fossilized tree resin)**

Insects and small animals were sometimes trapped in the resin when it was fresh and sticky. They were preserved inside as the amber hardened.

FOSSIL FECES

A piece of fossilized dung is called a coprolite. One of the longest coprolites ever found measured over 3.3 feet (1 m) long!

Cast

A cast fossil begins like a mold fossil with an imprint left in soft mud. Then, minerals build up in the space left behind and harden, creating a cast of the original shape.

Mold

An imprint of an animal or plant is left in soft mud, which later hardens into rock. The living thing decomposes but its imprint is left behind.

Trace fossil

These are fossils that provide evidence about how prehistoric animals lived, such as their footprints, nests, dung, and eggs.

QUIZ TIME!

After you've finished testing yourself, why not use this book to make a quiz to test your friends and family? You could take questions from each section to make different rounds, or mix and match across the book for a general-knowledge dinosaur quiz. You can even make up your own quiz questions! Use these dinosaur fossil facts to get you started. For example, **"What is a trace fossil?"** or **"Why are fossils of land animals rare?"**

ANSWERS

1 Birds
2 245 million years ago
3 66 million years ago
4 Bumpy, tough skin and some had feathers
5 A section of Earth's history based on the age of layers of sedimentary rock
6 *Charnia*
7 The Cambrian, Ordovician, Silurian, Devonian, Carboniferous, or the Permian
8 The Devonian Period
9 A synapsid (a mammal-like reptile)
10 A supercontinent of all the land on Earth during the Triassic Period
11 The Jurassic Period
12 201 to 145 million years ago
13 The Cretaceous Period
14 Around 300,000 years ago
15 Mexico
16 Disease, extreme volcanic activity, heatwaves, freezing temperatures, X-rays from a supernova star, or egg-eating mammals destroying high numbers of young
17 Bird-like dinosaurs and the ancestors of most mammals, crocodiles, turtles, and frogs
18 Saurischians and ornithischians
19 Carnivorous
20 Tyrant lizard
21 *Archaeopteryx*
22 98 feet (30 m) long
23 Ornithopod
24 For defense
25 Their back legs were much longer than their front legs, so they couldn't run on all fours
26 Skull
27 Horns and huge bony frills on the head
28 *Patagotitan*
29 60 feet (18 m)
30 A chicken
31 15
32 A lime
33 *Parasaurolophus*
34 As a trumpet to make sounds to communicate
35 Look at its teeth

36 Blade-like, serrated teeth
37 To grab fish out of the water
38 They worked like a rake to strip leaves off plants
39 *Edmontosaurus*
40 Because they constantly fell out and were replaced throughout their life
41 To help them digest tough plants
42 A predator at the top of the food chain with no natural predators
43 They had a giant hooked claw on each foot to grab prey and stop it from escaping
44 60 teeth
45 Their sense of smell
46 40 feet (12 m) long
47 Insects and small reptiles
48 Solid bone
49 By stabbing them with its large thumb spikes
50 Herbivorous (plants)
51 With spikes on its sides
52 Newborn dinosaurs hatched from eggs
53 Some were colored and patterned
54 8.8 pounds (4 kg)
55 20 inches (51 cm) long
56 By scanning them or by removing the shells with strong acid
57 That they came from giant birds
58 Open, or covered with soil, sand, or dead plants
59 They were safer
60 They fertilized the eggs
61 The yolk
62 Not for long, they were probably able to survive on their own as soon as they hatched
63 Where they went, how many dinosaurs traveled together, and the speed they traveled
64 By measuring the distance between the steps
65 *Diplodocus*
66 To protect them against predators
67 To bring down larger prey
68 *Coelophysis*
69 No, they were reptiles

70 Thin wings that stretched from the shoulder to the ankle
71 Small—around the size of a pigeon
72 33–39 feet (10–12 m)
73 The Cretaceous Period
74 Probably to attract a mate
75 20 inches (51 cm) long
76 A diamond-shaped rudder
77 66 million years ago, along with the dinosaurs
78 Ichthyosaurs
79 To spot predators
80 The Late Triassic Period
81 39–49 feet (12–15 m) long
82 A snake-like body with large, strong flippers and a long tail
83 The monitor lizard
84 Fish, ammonites, cuttlefish, and each other, especially young or weak animals
85 They were warm-blooded and gave birth to live young
86 Because they live in water and on land
87 The Devonian Period
88 With primitive lungs
89 It swam in the water and walked on land
90 To keep their skin moist and lay eggs
91 They grew scaly, dry skin and laid eggs with hard shells on land
92 6.6 feet (2 m) long
93 Fish and other small animals
94 The Triassic Period
95 The size of small rodents such as rats
96 To avoid reptile predators that were active during the day
97 Laying eggs, giving birth to very small young that live in pouches, or giving birth to developed young
98 They didn't need as much food and they had fur to keep them warm
99 In the last Ice Age, around 11,500 years ago
100 The sloth
101 11.5 feet (3.5 m) tall
102 Its armored tail with bony spikes

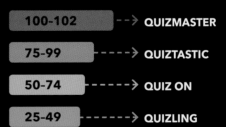

HOW WELL DID YOU DO?

100-102	- - ->	QUIZMASTER
75-99	- - - - ->	QUIZTASTIC
50-74	- - - - - ->	QUIZ ON
25-49	- - - - - - ->	QUIZLING
0-24	- - - - - - - ->	QUIZ IT AGAIN

GLOSSARY

amber Fossilized tree resin

ammonites Prehistoric sea creatures with flat, spiral shells

asteroid A large space rock that orbits the Sun

carnivores Animals that only eat meat

crater A bowl-shaped depression in the ground, usually caused by space rocks crashing into it

embryos Developing animals that are not ready to be born

eon A period of time that is so long it can't be measured

era A period of Earth's history based on the age of layers of sedimentary rock

evolve To change and develop gradually over time

fossils The shapes of things that have been preserved in rock for a very long time

gills The organs with which fish and some other water animals breathe

herbivores Animals that only eat plants

herds Large groups of animals that live and feed together

Ice Age A period of time during which the temperature on Earth dropped very low

invertebrate An animal without a backbone, such as an insect

mass extinction A period in which many species of living things die out forever

mate A reproductive partner

omnivores Animals that eat meat and plants

paleontologists People who study dinosaurs and prehistoric life

periods Lengths of time within an era

sediment Small pieces of sand, mud, and stones

sedimentary rock Rock that forms from layers of sediment being pressed together over a very long period of time

serrated Having a jagged edge like a saw

vertebrate An animal with a backbone, such as a fish or a mammal

warm-blooded Able to control its own body temperature and does not need to change environments to warm up or cool down

wingspan The distance between the tips of the wings of an animal

FURTHER INFORMATION

BOOKS

DK. *My Encyclopedia of Very Important Dinosaurs:*
Discover more than 80 prehistoric creatures.
DK Children, 2018.

Hyde, Natalie. *Dinosaur Fossils.*
Crabtree Publishing, 2014.

Lessem, Don. *Ultimate Dinopedia.*
National Geographic Kids, 2017.

WEBSITES

www.amnh.org/explore/ology/paleontology
Have fun learning more about dinosaurs with stories, games, and activities.

kids.nationalgeographic.com/search-results/?q=dinosaur
Find out more about dinosaurs and prehistoric animals. Then test your
memory with a dinosaur quiz.

www.dkfindout.com/us/dinosaurs-and-prehistoric-life/dinosaurs
Discover amazing facts and information about dinosaurs and prehistoric life.

INDEX